MW01713685

TEDDY 'N' ME

The Blitz And Other Childhood War Memories

by Peggy Halstead

FriesenPress

Suite 300 - 990 Fort St
Victoria, BC, Canada, V8V 3K2
www.friesenpress.com

First Edition — 2015

ISBN
978-1-4602-4596-5 (Hardcover)
978-1-4602-4597-2 (Paperback)
978-1-4602-4598-9 (eBook)

1. Biography & Autobiography, Personal Memoirs

Distributed to the trade by The Ingram Book Company

To Dave,

Without whom this book would not have been possible.

With love and gratitude

Table of Contents

PREFACE

During the 70s and into the early 80s I was doing a good deal of writing, mainly commentaries for CBC Radio, a number of short stories that appeared in a variety of family style journals, and three movie scripts. And then life overtook me, and my writing activity went into a quiet period.

However, in the back of my mind there was always a book waiting to be written about my time as a little girl in London growing up in the midst of the Second World War. This book lay dormant for years simply because, for one reason or other, I just couldn't get started. Then one Sunday I was listening to the Vinyl Cafe, a CBC Radio programme, and Stuart McLean, the host, told the story of one his characters Stephanie. Stephanie was a teenager who had just been to London to visit an elderly great-aunt. This upbeat, energetic senior wanted to have Stephanie experience as much of "her" London as possible and this, of course, included World War II. She told Stephanie about the air raids, the air raid shelters including those in the Underground stations and also told her about the war time parcels that had come to their house from a relative in Canada. Bingo! I knew that I had to write to Stuart and tell them about the wonderful parcels Mum's cousin

Rene had sent us, for four years running, containing all manner of food items which we couldn't get or which were in incredibly short supply. I wrote the letter and thought no more about it until just before Christmas 2007 I received a phone call from the producer of the Vinyl Cafe saying that Stuart loved my letter and he wanted to read it on his Christmas program that year. I was over the moon! His reading of my letter became the trigger for my writing ***Teddy "N" Me, The Blitz and other Childhood War Memories.***

I still needed the urging of my husband to get started, because I felt that there were only four or five stories that would have sufficient content to be put into a book format; that would not be enough. After all, I was just a year old when the war started and not quite seven when it ended. What could I have remembered? However, I soon discovered I was wrong. As I started to write, one story after another came to mind. In many ways it was like peeling an onion: one layer led to another. Some of the discoveries were funny and cute but many of them were very stressful and, like a peeled onion, caused tears to well up.

There have been a number of times in my adult life when something would happen that would generate an unexpected action or emotional response, a flashback perhaps, and often I would need help understanding why this was happening. These feelings were always connected to a childhood war experience. What I didn't bargain for was the sheer number and intensity of the emotional memories that came forward once I started to write them down. They had obviously been buried within me for decades. Once again I was I reliving the fears, anxieties, and uncertainties surrounding air raids, air raid sirens, V-1 Rockets (Buzz Bombs), V-2 Rockets, air raid shelters, evacuations, rationing and other wartime experiences. The little person that once was me had suddenly reappeared. Sometimes it was just too emotionally exhausting.

After the war was over my family didn't talk much about it except for the occasional story, mostly about people doing caring things for each other. I remembered the blackout wardens, a butcher, other shop keepers, the mean spirited old lady who owned the cottage that we lived in during one evacuation and the farm folk at the village market. They and others all played roles in how I remembered the war during the writing of *Teddy 'N' Me*.

Unfortunately I couldn't remember very much of my Dad because he was in uniform and away nearly the entire time. I do remember a great deal about my two grandmothers because we lived in side by side terraces and we were in daily contact. And of course I remembered my Mum because she and Teddy were my constant companions.

I now understand how the war has affected my life some 70 years later.

The writing of *Teddy 'N' Me* has been at times a troubling emotional experience. It has also been highly rewarding, however, because it has allowed me to truly appreciate the mental fibre and resourcefulness of my two grandmothers and my mother.

I hope that everyone who reads *Teddy 'N' Me*, including political and community leaders, will gain a deeper understanding of what the life of a child was like during these stressful war times and will also look around the world and realize that there are thousands upon thousands of children who are currently living in horrific war conditions. My heart goes out to them as I know that in their years to come they are likely to wrestle with their childhood experiences over and over again.

Finally, to you the reader: I hope you will enjoy the stories and take meaning from them.

Peggy (Collins) Halstead

MY SPECIAL THANKS GO TO:

The Late Peter Gzowski,
Host of *This Country in the Morning,*
Morningside and *The Morningside Papers.*

Stuart McLean
Host and star of *The Vinyl Cafe*

Jess Milton
Producer of *The Vinyl Cafe*

The Saskatchewan Writers Guild

Sask Film

Sharon Butala,
For all your invaluable support and encouragement.

Last, but not least, a big thank you to my sisters-in-law, Margaret Speers and Karen Pryznyk, and brother-in-law Grant Pryznyk for reading and rereading the manuscript and searching out "the little writer's gremlins" which had found their way onto some of the pages. Thanks also to Brenda McKenzie for her wonderful drawings for two of the stories.

Family

TEDDY

The *Teddy* of the title refers to the teddy bear given to me for my first birthday by one of my grandfathers.

He was a typical teddy bear of that time: glass eyes, unbendable but movable arms and legs, all held together by a linkage of wires which couldn't be felt but which made replacing one of the eyes a difficult feat, although my mother tried to accomplish this on several occasions. He also had a stitched nose and leather patches on his paws and feet and is now almost bald around the middle.

I immediately fell in love with him. He became my most precious possession; but more than that he was security, my rock, my everything. I took him everywhere — into air raid shelters, on trains and buses, and to the evacuation cottages.

People came and went, but Teddy was always there. Over the course of the years and our many experiences Teddy has required reconstructive surgery to reattach his right ear and to firm up his neck muscles; his right eye is missing and his left nose whiskers are gone. But he is still with me.

Many years later — many, many years later — my son-in-law brought my granddaughter into the room where I keep Teddy on a high shelf. She took one look and wanted him. Her father gave him to her and she threw her arms around and hugged him just the way I used to. Her hugs, and all of mine, probably explain why Teddy's tummy fur is worn away.

Teddy

MY FAMILY

My family consisted of Mum, Dad, and me. Dad was called up as soon as war broke out. I only saw him five or six times for the duration of the war. As a result we had a poor relationship and never really bonded.

He worked on the Southern Railway from the age of fourteen, and shortly before the war became eligible for a small flat in Folkstone Gardens owned by the railway. When I was very young we lived in a house in Rupack Street near the entrance of the Rotherhithe Tunnel, it had heavy green painted shutters, which

I would go out and help Mum to close every night. Since I could barely reach them, helping was a very loose term.

Dad, Mum and Me

I also had four grandparents: Granddad and Nanny Cocks were Mum's parents. Granddad Cocks was a small, jolly man who was always smiling, or so it seemed to me. Not that he had much to smile about: he had worked on the docks as a stevedore until, fed up with the appalling working conditions, he tried to organize a union. He was promptly sacked and was blacklisted, which meant he could no longer work on the docks.

Granddad Cocks was a conscientious objector during the First World War and was posted to an Army Hospital in St. Petersburg, Russia. The hospital was a magnificent requisitioned palace which boasted a huge marble staircase that was fronted by a three story, floor to ceiling, stained glass window. One winter's day Granddad was carrying an armload of medical stuff down this staircase. The staircase was damp, his foot slipped and he skidded down the last few steps across the landing and crashed out through the stained glass window. During the Depression he tried to apply for a job with the Town Council; there was just one job advertised but five hundred men turned up for it. Granddad turned up early and was one of the first in the queue. Unfortunately, when the doors opened there was such a crush of people pushing to get in that he tripped and fell. Two men who were at the head of the queue turned back to pull him up, probably saving his life but losing their chance at the job.

Nan Cocks' Father and Grandfather both served as captains on sailing ships, going around Cape Horn under sail — considered the greatest feat of seamanship in the world.

My Granddad Collins, a highly skilled cobbler in civilian life, was quite different, tall with a military bearing and a large moustache. He was an intimidating figure and quite formal. An example of his demeanour occurred one afternoon while I was lying on the floor cutting up newspapers, when he came in and said, "You'd better clear that up before Nanny comes home." When I mentioned this to Mum, many years later she burst out laughing and said, "You want to know what he really said to you? He said clear that mess up before *Mrs. Collins* comes home."

He served in the Army for several years and was part of the British Expeditionary Force which was sent to Khartoum to rescue General Gordon who was besieged there. Unfortunately they arrived too late and were greeted by the sight of Gordon's head on a pike on the city walls. Rather than being sent home, they were then ordered on to fight in the Boer War. They sailed down (or was it *up*) the Nile. This was a Collins family joke.

Both my grandfathers died early in the war.

This seemed to set a trend for the Collins family. My father was based in Algeria at the end of the war, my husband and I and our two children spent two plus years in Ghana while Dave worked for CIDA (Canadian International Development Agency), and our daughter won a two-week trip to Morocco when our grandson was only four months old, making him the fifth generation to end up in Africa. He was slightly more willing to be there than many of the others in my family.

I also had a Great Grandmother Edmonds who had raised both Mum and her cousin Rene from birth. The last time I saw her I was very small and she was living in a hospital. She was a very imposing looking lady in a long black dress with a frilled cap on her head and a full white apron.

MY UNCLE LES

Les was 11½ years older than I and about twelve and half years old when the war broke out. He received his call up notice on the day the war ended. He often said, in jest, that when the enemy knew he'd joined the army they just gave up.

During the war years my Mum and I lived almost continuously with Nan Cocks and him except for the few times Dad was on leave or when we were evacuated. In my mind Les was not really my uncle but rather a super big brother.

One thing that stuck in my mind about Les was that he almost always had a job. He was smart, reliable, and would turn his hand to any work possibility. Les had some interesting jobs around this time. One involved taking the huge Clydesdale horses from the stables to the farrier to be shod. These were the horses that pulled the brewer's drays to deliver beer kegs to the pubs. The horses were cheaper and more effective to use than lorries because they didn't use petrol (gas) and lorries were scarce and needed for the war effort. Les would get up really early before school and walk to the stables somewhere on Tower Bridge Road and then ride one of the horses bareback to the farrier's, located along Jamaica Road, while leading one or two others.

Good thing they were gentle creatures in spite of their size. However, one in particular was very skittish and took every opportunity to turn tail and run for the comfort of his stable. Les tried to take just this one horse for shoeing at a time but often he was told to take more than one and if it ran away he'd wait for a tram to come along. The driver would stop and tell Les where he'd seen the horse then carry on his route until he met the tram coming in the other direction. He would then tell that driver about Les, and this second driver would stop and pick up Les and take him back to where his run away horse was waiting. In the meantime Les would have tied his other horses to a tree, all the iron railings having been removed to be used in the war effort.

The horses, like the residents in the area, got very nervous in the bombing raids and had to be sent off regularly to a farm deep in the country where they could eat green grass, rest, and do natural 'horsey' things. One of the newspapers would often do a "good news story," with photos, about these huge horses frolicking about on their vacation.

Another job Les had, probably after he left school, was as a mechanic in a garage near Deptford High Street. One day the air raid siren went off and with almost no warning the bombs started to fall. There was no air raid shelter nearby so Les and his co-worker dove under the lorry they were working on and with their hands over their ears waited out the raid. After the raid, the garage owner came out and said, "Wot do you two idiots think you're doing?" Les and his friend replied, "We're sheltering under this lorry from the bombs." The owner burst out laughing and asked, "What lorry?" When they looked up, the lorry was gone.

It had been lifted off them by the blast of a bomb that had landed nearby and had been blown across the road.

I still smile when I imagine what the garage owner saw, two teens lying on their stomachs, flat on the ground, fully exposed but thinking they were, in some way, protected.

Uncle Les

The Blitz, Air Raid Sirens, Ack-Ack Guns, and Air Raid Shelters

SOUTHWARK PARK

Our street, Matson Street, was a little one off Southwark Park Road. My Nan's houses were side by side and we often said we should knock a hole in one of the adjoining walls and be able to go between the two houses with ease. The nicest thing about them was that they backed onto Southwark Park. This is a huge park which has beautiful flower beds, large lawns, was well treed, and had a paddling pool for children like me. In addition, there used to be a small lake, but it took a bomb hit and for reasons I don't understand was never able to hold water again.

At one edge of the park is St. James Church and in 1921 a wonderful slide was built on the church grounds and given to the children of the area by a Mr. Carr of Peak Freens. My family has reason to believe that one of the boys in the photo of the grand opening was my father. This was one of my most favourite places to play and many years later I was able to take my children to enjoy this happy piece of my childhood.

Until recently the park had a major road running though it. This divided the park into two sides and when war broke out the half behind our houses was taken over by the military.

That area was used as a base for Ack-Ack (anti-aircraft) guns. These were huge guns which made a terrific pounding noise. They could be swung around on their base so that they could track the planes overhead. There was a battery of search lights, and this area was also the home of a barrage balloon base. These were large balloons that were floated aloft on wires and were designed to prevent low flying aircraft from bombing the guns, nearby houses, shops, and the nearby docks which were stacked with wood from around the world.

My favourite book at the time was called *Blossom, the Barrage Balloon* which told the story of a balloon that broke away from her base and chased down an enemy plane for which she received a medal. I loved that book, but didn't realize how the memories of the balloons had left such an impression on me until one day not too long ago I was driving to a town south of Winnipeg. We came around a bend in the road and I came face to face with a barrage balloon. It was like getting punched in the stomach and I almost ran off the road. Even though it had been sixty years or more since I'd seen one it still had the power to shock. Ever since whenever we drive to this town my husband warns me if the balloon is flying.

Slide in St. James Churchyard

AIR RAIDS AND AIR RAID SHELTERS

My Nan Collins got two air raid shelters. I don't know if she had to pay for them, but I do know the government encouraged everyone to get at least one; as I was little, no one told me anything. There was one for the outside, called an Anderson shelter, which was partially dug into the ground and covered by sheets of corrugated iron with dirt and sod piled on top. It was small, cramped, damp, and uncomfortable but it would withstand almost everything except a direct hit.

It was the second one known as a Morrison shelter that really scared me, because it was built with flat, widely-spaced steel bars placed about a foot apart, and was for use indoors. I was afraid of it because I knew that in the case of a hit there was a great chance of fire; most people cooked by gas and the smallest spark could start a fire. I tried to tell Mum what I was afraid of, but I probably lacked the vocabulary to properly describe my fears and she was too stressed to take the time to explain that the shelter was designed to protect us in case the house collapsed. At any rate I was ignored and took all my naps in the Morrison shelter, which was set up in the front room.

We made a lot of use of the Anderson shelter even though it was cramped, cold, damp, and dirty. We never used it unless the air raid siren sounded. One night I was getting ready for bed and Mum was applying a poultice to a large boil on my face. Suddenly the dreaded air raid siren went off. Immediately everyone started scurrying around collecting things we needed to take out to the shelter. I felt something running down my face and called Mum to tell her the boil had broken. It took awhile to get her attention but everyone else went to the shelter while Mum hurriedly tried to clean up the mess. I still have a small scar on my face from that incident.

It must have been very upsetting to my Mum that her mother, Nan Cocks, flatly refused on most occasions to go to any shelter at all, stating firmly that "No blankety, blank German is going to force me out of my house."

Anderson Shelter

Courtesy: Winton Community Forum

In 2008 my husband and I went to the UK to visit relatives. While in London, we took my Aunt Olive to see an exhibition at the Imperial War Museum called "Children of War." Since she is only 11 years older than me we both had a vested interest in seeing it. Ultimately, we were disappointed in the sanitized view of the war experiences we and other children endured. The exhibition included an exhibit called "The Blitz," which was supposed to give people the experience of a night in an Air Raid shelter. As we went in the air raid siren went off, Aunt Olive and I both clapped our hands over our ears causing the guide at the door to exclaim worriedly "Are you both OK?"

"The Blitz" exhibition, too, was a very sanitized version. There a gentle thump and a shake of the bench on which we were sitting, both supposed to represent a bomb strike, and I automatically hunched my shoulders against the falling debris, insects, and dirt which I unconsciously expected to fall from the roof of the shelter. Of course it didn't happen at the museum but although I hadn't thought of that from the last day of the war, the depiction brought the experience back in vivid detail.

TEDDY AND THE AIR RAID

It happened early in the war, right at the beginning of the Blitz. At the time we were living on the top floor of a three story block of flats, there were six or seven similar blocks lined up and known collectively as Folkestone Gardens. They were poorly positioned from a safety point of view because they were right next to major railway lines that ran from Central London to many of the towns and cities on the South Coast of England and those in between. On the other side of the road was a stretch of above-ground Underground (subway) railway. In addition, the flats were only a few miles from the London docks, among them Canada Wharf and Canary Wharf, which were piled high with lumber from Canada and around the world. This made the whole area ideal targets for the German air force, the *Luftwaffe*, who were determined to set the whole city on fire.

On this particular night I awoke in a fright when my father snatched me from my bed, wrapped me in a blanket, and prepared to carry me outside to the air raid shelter in the quadrangle below. I protested. I wanted my Teddy, and Dad turned back to grab him.

The block was shaking with the concussion of falling and exploding bombs. The noise was terrible with the drone of plane engines, the booms and flashes from anti-aircraft guns, the patter of shrapnel clattering on the building's roof and into the courtyard below and the persistent whine of the air raid siren.

Too terrified to cry, I clung to my dad and of course, Teddy. The staircase was stone and slippery. One flight of stairs led down to a landing that was open to the outside while the next flight led into complete darkness to the front doors of two flats on the floor below us. There was no lighting — the blackout was strictly enforced — the only light came from the flashes of the Ack-Ack guns, the searchlights sweeping across the skies and explosions from bombs falling nearby.

We were almost at the bottom of the second flight when the unthinkable happened — Dad slipped on the second to last step and as he struggled to keep his balance in the pitch blackness and not to drop me, Teddy was jerked from my arms and fell to the floor.

I lost it. I burst into tears, crying for Teddy. Dad tried to reassure me that we'd get him on the way back upstairs but I wouldn't be calmed, begging Dad to turn on the torch so we could find him. Eventually, he did so and in the brief flash of light we spotted the poor little bear and he was quickly picked up and thrust into my arms. During this family drama the fighting overhead had increased in ferocity and Dad decided it was too dangerous to try to get to the air raid shelter that was located between two facing blocks of flats, so we returned to our flat. We sat on the floor in the corridor, that being the safest place in the flat. I was snuggled between my parents, wrapped in a blanket and clutching my Teddy.

I woke up in my bed in the morning; in the flat the signs of the savagery of the night before were that all the windows at the back of our flat were blown in. The block of flats two doors down received a direct hit.

It just got worse from there. The Blitz went on for eight long months with both daylight and nighttime raids until the RAF got the upper hand. Then the raids became more sporadic but just as terrifying.

Then came the V-1s (aka Buzz Bombs or Doodlebugs). These unmanned V-1s droned over the cities until their engines cut out.

In some ways the V-1s were almost a joke, except of course for the people who were hit. Their guidance systems were erratic, to say the least, with the rockets shooting off in all directions and crashing into unintended targets. Some of them even turned around and, like homing pigeons, headed back towards the factory where they were built. There was a strong rumour that the slave labourers who were forced to build the guidance systems deliberately sabotaged them, preferring to die themselves rather than kill others.

Nineteen years later I immigrated to Winnipeg, Canada. Winnipeg is a city of bridges as two rivers, one from the south, the Red, and one from the west, the Assiniboine, meet to flow north, ultimately to Hudson's Bay. For most of my first 15 months in Canada, I lived in Winnipeg, worked north of the Assiniboine, and lived south of it. Frequently I crossed a bridge where a significant portion of the surface was an iron grid or grating. Every time I crossed the bridge I would experience an uncomfortable shiver and I would tense up but I didn't know why. When my Mum came out a month or so before my wedding, I mentioned this to her. "Oh," she said, "that sounds just like the unmanned Buzz Bombs."

For those of you who have experienced the sound of car tires crossing one of these steel grids, you will recall that suddenly there is deep drone, that really is more of a growl, and then suddenly that sound stops once the car moves onto a smooth concrete or tarmac surface. During a Buzz Bomb attack, we would suddenly hear the drone of the bomb; then the bomb's engine would cut out, the drone would stop, and we had to wait for the bomb to drop and explode. Everyone lived a lifetime waiting for the explosion which told us we had survived another attack.

Sound, then agonizing silence! Obviously I had retained the emotional memories and tensions of the Buzz Bombs but not the other details.

CHEESMANS & THE BOMB

One day Mum decided to go to Lewisham where there was a large street market lined with stalls selling fruits and vegetables as well as clothing and household goods. There were also several large shops, C&As and Marks & Spencer, among others. It was quite a long bus ride, which I enjoyed since I loved sitting on the top deck of the double-decker bus.

Someone on the bus announced "There's no point going to Cheesmans, it got a direct hit last night." We had to walk past Cheesmans on our way to the market. It didn't look good as there was glass all over the pavement from the shattered windows but there was seemingly little apparent damage apart from the four-faced clock tower that stood in the middle of the intersection and it appeared to have taken the brunt of the bomb blast.

On our way back to get the bus we saw a hastily hand lettered sign hanging across a couple of Cheesmans ground floor windows, reading "Open for Business." We crossed the street and were directed to a door further down the street. Inside, we found most of the departments open and shop assistants sweeping up and dusting the glass topped and sided counters. We were invited to go to the main part of the shop which contained several floors. The upper floors were roped off but all else seemed normal.

The oddest thing about Cheesmans was that there was an underground walkway which passed under a street and connected to another portion of the store. I didn't like using this corridor as the ceiling was low and lined with overhead pipes; the good part about it was that it led to the children's toy department, not that there were very many to see and most were quite expensive too.

One year Mum took me to the toy department to see Father Christmas; he was a terrible grump and scowled at all the children who came to see him. A large sign said "Every child will receive a gift." Mum thought it was a good idea so she led me through the line. I was too shy to talk to him and he was very intimidating. He thrust the gift at me and called "Next!" The gift was a pencil, unsharpened, in a tiny knitted sock tied up with a piece of ribbon.

Wow! Merry Christmas from Cheesmans.

The Evacuations

THE FIRST EVACUATION

Some time in 1941 during the Blitz, Mum agreed to be evacuated; everyone had been trying to persuade her to go somewhere, anywhere out of London but, I think, due to Nanny Cocks' flat refusal to move, she wouldn't go.

Finally the constant bombing, my screaming, and the fact that Nanny Collins had already left with her daughter, my Aunt Olive, persuaded her. Olive was old enough to go on her own but Nan was widowed and was allowed to go too. Mum refused to let me go alone; I was about three and just young enough to qualify for company.

A lot of the children who went alone were abused. A friend of mine was the same age as me but because she had a brother to go with her, her mother wasn't allowed to. She had gorgeous red hair that had never been cut and was almost to her waist. Unfortunately, no one would take them because of a superstition in the village over red hair and the person who was finally persuaded to take them promptly cut all her hair off.

Fortunately, we were assigned to the same village as my Nan, now widowed, and Aunt Olive and Nan was able to persuade the lady who had the farm house they were living in to take us in too.

It was a little village near Oxford named Great Milton. Whenever I think of Great Milton I think of sunshine and fun, even though I know it was far from that. But for one thing there were no air raids, no sirens, no dashes to the air raid shelters. For the first while, it was heaven. We lived in a large farm house which was warm! I think it must have had some form of central heating, and to me it was bliss. We, Mum and I, went for long walks down the country lanes; sometimes I was allowed to take the two dogs in the house for a walk too. One was a little Scottish Terrier (Scotty) and the other was a Great Dane (Dusty) which was taller than me. Fortunately he was very gentle and walked very well for me despite Mum's concerns.

Landlord, Scotty, Dusty and Me

Dusty and Me

Nan Collins, Aunt Olive, Scotty and Me

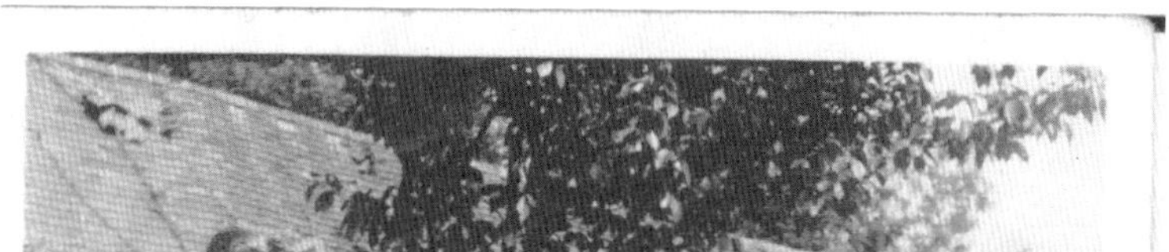

Mum, Nan Collins and Me and other Evacuees

One day we were out for a walk along a stream, when suddenly I saw a flash of the most brilliant azure blue. "What was that?" I gasped. Mum explained it was a kingfisher. I've never seen one since but I'll never forget the sight of that brilliant blue. Another time with were walking past the water mill; it wasn't working that day so the miller came out and invited us in to see the workings of the mill. He showed us the two huge grindstones; they made such a terrible noise as they revolved against each other. I didn't like being in the mill; the sounds, the dust, and the general atmosphere were all too much for me so we seldom went back, but I always thought how very nice of the miller to invite us to see the mill.

The landlady kept rabbits to supplement their food supply. One day the rabbits all escaped from their hutches, and there was great flurry of activity to round up the bunnies and get them out of the vegetable garden and back into their hutches. The rabbits had been really enjoying themselves. Finally when all the rabbits were safely back in their hutches the conversation turned to how had the rabbits escaped? The puzzle was soon solved when I was caught looking very angelic but unlatching one of the hutches.

Great Milton was also, the scene of my first proposal. I, being three, accepted but neither of us knew what to do next, so we just sort of drifted around ignoring each other.

Once the bombing abated a little Mum decided to go back to London. I think she really missed her Mum and I wasn't really company enough for her so back we went. I, of course, had no say in the matter. We moved back in with Nan Cocks and Uncle Les.

THE SECOND EVACUATION

The second evacuation was quite different to the first even though we went back to Great Milton. Unfortunately, the lady who had taken us in the first time had no room for us and we were billeted in a cottage in the village. The lady who had the cottage was old (I must have been a great trial to her) and very stern, with an imperious manner, and she treated Mum like some hired help. Her maid had left to do war work and she was very resentful of the fact.

On one of the rare occasions Dad got leave to come and see us she insisted he pick the apples on the old apple tree whose branches stretched out over the pigstye at the end of the garden. Her gardener had refused to pick them because he was afraid of the stye's only resident, a huge, bad tempered boar. Dad protested he couldn't pick the apples because he was in uniform (he only had 24 hours leave). But she wouldn't take no for an answer, so the gardener produced a large ladder and Dad climbed up. The first few apples were easy but she stood by the fence exhorting him not to drop any into the stye. She was most insistent that none be dropped, all the while the boar hung around under the tree waiting. I was on tenterhooks worried about Dad falling into the stye or dropping an apple. Finally, there was just one apple left, it dangled enticingly at the very end of a branch which stretched out over the stye just out of reach of the boar. Dad started down the ladder refusing to go after it but she stood at the foot of the ladder ordering him back up again. Finally, he cautiously reached out along the branch and grasped the apple, all the while being told not to drop it. He was carefully edging back when — the apple popped out of his hand and fell into the stye where it was promptly pounced upon and gobbled up in a flash by the boar. I never did find out whether it was an accident or whether Dad felt sorry for the boar and had dropped it deliberately.

There was a town not too far away called Thame, which was rumoured to be the headwaters of the Thames river. I used to look for it (the headwaters) but never did find it. The main attraction was that every so often there would be a farmer's market held. It was very popular because the farmers could sell their produce "at the gate" rather than having to have permits to sell goods on the open market. We would take a bus which went around the country lanes and took ages to get to Thame. It would make unscheduled stops along the way to pick up farmer's wives laden with baskets of produce of various kinds.

There were also many pens for animals, and one day there was great excitement in the wide main street when a small pig got out of his pen and took off at top speed down the street, chased by every small boy in the vicinity. Of course also by the owner who was frantically trying to catch the pig and yelling to everyone to stop it. I had great sympathy for the pig and really hoped it would get away, but a while later I saw the farmer returning up the street with the pig tucked firmly under his arm.

Thame's Market

The home we were staying in was a solid, double-fronted cottage. There was a large pantry all lined with slate and smelling delightfully of milk and dairy produce. We had a bedroom upstairs which was very cold and where water ran down the walls in the summer and mushrooms proliferated on the walls in the winter.

One time it was decided to hold a fancy dress parade for the children to boost morale. I wanted to enter of course and Mum racked her brains trying to think of something she could rustle up for me to wear. With all the shortages it seemed impossible until the day someone in the village suggested I wear a Hungarian dress she had. It was a lovely thing covered in embroidery and with stiff petticoats to hold out the skirts. I was very disappointed when my Mother declared it to be large enough to go over my coat. But I enjoyed the party, didn't win of course, but I felt like a princess in my lovely dress. It was easily the most elaborate thing I'd ever seen.

One of the most interesting things about the cottage we were in was that in a corner of the garden was another garden surrounded by a high wall. It had intricate paved paths through it, but most intriguing of all was a fountain in the centre of the garden. It was filled with green, scummy water but every one told me it would be fixed up after the war. In fact the whole garden was in a sad state of disrepair; probably the old gardener found it all too much to cope with, but I loved it. I had just listened to "The Secret Garden" by Frances Hodgson Burnett, which had been serialized on a children's program on the BBC. I was sure this was *the* Secret Garden that was being written about. I was forbidden to go into the garden alone but spent hours peering through the elaborate iron gate at the entrance, wishing I could stroll the paths and sit by the fountain.

PLANES, GLIDERS. WHAT WAS GOING ON?

We were evacuated in Autumn of 1944 and one day while taking our usual walk a few planes flew over. Then the planes increased in number — all kinds of planes including more and more gliders (light, engineless planes made of balsa wood, which were towed by larger powered planes). Once they were released from their tow lines they "rode the thermals" until they landed. The pilots became very skilled in riding these invisible columns of air and could travel long distances using them. Soon the sky was black with them and the sun was nearly blotted out. Mum looked up at the sky and said, "Something is going on." I asked, "What is it?" even though I knew better. Adults never told children anything.

Later we heard a glider had crashed in field just outside the village and we decided to go and see it. It was guarded by two young airmen, one wing was crushed from the landing but apart from that it looked fine, although the airmen told us it would probably be scrapped. No one had been hurt in the crash and they said everything would have been fine had the field been smoother. As it was, the wing had caught a rut and crumpled.

I was very interested because my Dad was in the RAF, although I didn't know what he did or where he was. All the small boys from the village were running around pestering the airmen with requests to go inside the glider. "No," was the answer, but one of the airmen broke off a small piece of the wing and gave it to me. I still have it.

Learning About Canada

VISITORS FROM CANADA

One day there was great excitement in the house. A letter had come from Rene. It contained news of her life on the farm and her children but the most exciting part told us that her brother-in-law Bert, had been called up and was being posted to England and she had asked him to come and see us if he possibly could. Mum was excited because she expected he would bring more news of Rene and her family.

It was a cold and windy day. My legs were chapped and sore and I was glad to get home from another of our customary long walks around the shops. It was a great surprise when we did get back to the house one day to find two large men in the back room talking to my grandmother. I wasn't used to men being around, so I was very shy and hid in the kitchen until curiosity got the better of me and I edged around the door to see what was going on. Mum and Nan were talking to the two uniformed men. They both ignored me but one of them was fiddling with something in his hat. Something that clinked and rattled, intrigued I crept closer and closer until I was standing next to him and able to see he was playing with some coins.

That broke the ice and we soon became friends. He explained he was Rene's brother-in-law Bert and his friend was from somewhere in Canada called Québec. I was shy with him too at first but I loved his way of speaking and his musical French Canadian accent. They came a few times afterwards, the French Canadian man telling my grandmother that they "made the daughter the excuse to visit the mother."

One day they came in and stood in the back room still wearing their hats. This was unusual, I'd never seen them wearing their hats in the house before; normally they took them off at the door.

This time they waited until Mum and I were in the back room then they stood in front of my grandmother, both bowed low, and swept their hats off in a great flourish. We were all laughing at their antics until we noticed something in their hats and the laughter changed to "Oohs," for nestled in each cap was an egg! Mum and Nan were very impressed — I'd never seen an egg before so I was less interested. I thought eggs came in the form of the dried egg powder we got with our rations.

When the excitement died down they explained they had gone to the camp cook and asked for some food for us. The cook grumbled that if he gave food to all the soldiers who asked for it he would soon be feeding the entire population of London and soon run out of supplies. Apparently a large number of Canadian troops had been asking for food that day. He grumbled and grumbled but finally produced two eggs. Bert and his friend protested that they had no way of carrying fresh eggs without breaking them, to which the cook replied "Are you daft? Put 'em in yer 'ats!"

They only came once after that to tell us they were being posted overseas and so were confined to barracks from now on. Bert came back to Canada but I don't know about his friend.

Rene was disappointed that the only thing Bert ever told her about us in one of his letters was how shocked he was at the conditions we were living in. I think that comment was the trigger for the parcels Rene sent us.

RENE'S CHRISTMAS PARCELS

Irene was my Mum's cousin. She and my Mum were, as little girls, raised as sisters by their grandmother since both of their mothers had to work. They were only a year apart in age and emotionally remained close all through their lives. Somehow for my Mum and then later for me 'Irene' was shortened to 'Rene,' pronounced (Renee). When Rene was about 13 her Mummy, my Great Aunt Annie and my Nan, her sister, had a spat over goodness knows what and Aunt Annie and Rene immigrated to Canada. Rene later married a farmer and she and her family lived on farm in Manitoba, Canada. Since they had been great friends as children my Mum and Rene had been able to stay in touch even though their lives were very different.

And now for the story of what became known as "Rene's parcels." These precious parcels arrived for four straight years in the middle of November.

The first one arrived while we, Mum and I, had been out for a walk. That was what you did during the war, walked around all the shops to see if they had anything — food or anything else to buy. People would queue up in front of shops if there was a chance there might be something to buy. One time Mum and I joined a queue and then asked the lady in front of us what was being queued for. The lady didn't know. It was important, to a certain degree, to patronize one or two local shops because they might give you a preference when certain goods came in. One time we met a lady who was carrying a few bananas Mum asked where she had got then and immediately went into that shop. The shop assistant denied having had any bananas for sale for months. This was untrue but she was taking care of her regular customers.

When we got home, tired and cold, my grandmother said a parcel had come from Rene for us. It was in the front room and when we opened the door we were enveloped in a rush of cold air (coal was rationed so we had heat in only one room) and a wonderful smell of pine. When I asked Mum what it was she said it was from all the pine trees in Canada and for years that was how I thought of this country: cold and pine trees. The parcel was carefully sewn in a flour sack which Mum painstakingly unpicked stitch by stitch while I danced with impatience waiting for her to get to the contents. She later made the sacks into tea towels, aprons, & pillow cases. I was about three plus at the time and I'd heard about the wonderful Christmas presents wrapped in colourful paper that would come my way when the war was over so to me the parcel contained all the "riches of Araby" wrapped up in a flour sack.

Eventually, Mum got the sack, covered in colourful stamps, unpicked and began to carefully open the cardboard box inside. By now even my grandmother was caught up in the excitement. Although she and Rene's mother had "had words" years ago, and

I sensed she disapproved of the parcel, curiosity got the better of her.

Finally Mum opened the box and instead of the "riches of Araby" wrapped in coloured paper there was food! I was a bit disappointed until Mum began removing the contents, she and my grandmother exclaiming over every item. There was a Christmas cake laden with dried fruit, something I'd never seen, and a one pound bag of sugar — more sugar than we'd had at one time since rationing started.

The parcels always contained so many things that were rationed, in short supply, or just unobtainable, often things I'd never seen. There was always one small present for me: a comic book, a leather bag, a pair of fancy hair slides (barrettes) that were so unusual that people would stop Mum in the street to ask where she had got them.

One year there was a chicken in a glass jar — a wonder indeed. As Mum took it out of the box she said "Here's our Christmas dinner," and it was. Together with the Christmas pudding it made a festive meal. The bottled chicken was a great hit. The meat was full of flavour, moist, tender, and covered in a delicious jelly.

Oh was that jelly ever good! I wanted to eat it all myself but, of course, I had to share it with everyone else.

Mum, Me, Nan Cocks, and one of Rene's wonderful Christmas parcels

Then there was the year customs opened the box, the first and only time it happened. They included a nice note telling us they had searched the parcel but in the search they cut open the paper bag of sugar. Oh, they put it in another bag and put it back of course, but some had spilled all over the box and its contents. Mum spread a cloth on the table and wiped all the sugar off each item then she carefully flattened the box and shook each grain of sugar into a bowl, going over each seam and fold time and time again to make sure no grains were missed — all the while with tears pouring down her face at the unfairness of it all.

Mum cried again at the end of the war when Rene wrote to say she'd heard that things were back to normal in the UK now that the war was over and she didn't think we needed any more parcels. I wanted Mum to write and tell Rene that far from being back to normal conditions were still dreadful. But Mum explained that the cost of the food and the postage were probably too expensive for Rene to send so we wrote and thanked Rene for all her help instead.

I came to visit Rene and her family many years ago. I later moved to Canada, met my husband and have been here ever since.

When Rene passed away a few years ago instead of flowers I placed on her grave a small box wrapped in Christmas paper. I got a few odd looks but Rene, my Mum, and I knew what it meant.

During the war I saw a newsreel clip of a Merchant Marine convoy sailing into Murmansk Harbour. The ships were unrecognizable as ships so covered in thick ice were they that they resembled icebergs more than ships. Before they could dock, men with big axes boarded the ships and hacked away at the ice with the axes. The commentary described the difficulties of the voyage: U-Boats, mines, the weather, before mentioning that the cargo included mail and parcels from Canada to the U.K. I have always felt a deep debt of gratitude to the men of the Merchant Marine who risked their lives to bring Rene's parcels to us.

The People, Their Lives on Matson and Neighbouring Streets

OUR HOUSE ON MATSON STREET

The council houses in Matson Street were terraces in the classic, two up-two down working class dwelling format. Each house had two bedrooms upstairs and a front room and back room downstairs. Ours had a tiny separate kitchen with a cooker, cold water tap over a stoneware sink and one cupboard. Perhaps these could have been called "two up-two and a bit down" instead. These terraces were considered to be one step up on the tenements and were probably built in the early 1900s.

The toilet/loo was a water closet outside in the back garden which was reached by going out the back door, walking down the garden path and turning left. The coal bin or coal house was also outside and just to the right of kitchen door. This was how Nan Cocks' house was laid out; Nan Collins and Aunt Olive's house was the same except left-right reversed. Plus they had an Anderson air raid shelter in the middle of their backyard.

There was a belief that the designers of these houses had the feeling that working class people would not make good use of a bathtub and would probably store coal in it, so bath tubs were omitted. Bathing was done in a tin tub in front of the back room fireplace. The front and the back rooms could be heated by coal fireplaces; there was no heat in the bedrooms or the kitchen.

The term, 'two up-two down' is so ingrained in British lexicon that it often becomes an element of humour. We were back in London a few years ago and were taking a stroll through Regent's Park when we came upon a number of Bobbies patrolling a fenced area and a great deal of joyous partying going on the other side of the fence. We asked a Bobbie what was happening and he replied. "Oh the US Ambassador has a little *two up-two down* in there and he is hosting a Fourth of July celebration."

Nan Cocks and Mum at #16 Matson Street

WASHDAY ON MATSON STREET

Each street was its own little community and each street had its little rituals; for the most part people didn't move round very much.

Mondays were always washing days. According to an unspoken agreement the first lady to get her washing done and hung out on the clothes line was the 'winner" for that week. Unlike today, doing the washing was hard work. First the water had to be carried from the sink to the boiler. Then the water had to be heated, using the gas fire underneath the boiler. While the water was heating the clothes were sorted. Whites were washed first, then colours, and finally the work clothes.

Clothes washing was not only hard physical work it had to be done with care and skill. First the clothes were washed in the hot soapy water, then mangled and run into the rinse water, rinsed and mangled again, and finally hung on the clothesline to dry. Mangling the clothes wasn't easy; it wasn't just a matter of shoving clothes in between the heavy rollers. If shirts were fed into the mangle at the wrong angle the buttons would pop off the garment, often ripping the clothes in the process.

I used to wear something called a liberty bodice and I hated them. They were sleeveless and it was my arms that were always cold. But my Mother insisted so of course I wore them. They were made of heavy material, something like the corsets Mum wore. But the worst thing was the rubber buttons that did up the front of the bodice. They were difficult to handle or do up, especially for little fingers. Why they had to be made of rubber I'll never know. When being washed the buttons were apt to pop off, sometimes to disappear into the murky depths of the washing water. Whether these buttons were found again really didn't matter because they were impossible to reattach, though Mum did try on several occasions.

As for the sheets they were often "top and tailed" or turned top to bottom, or even turned over getting a few extra days (or weeks)of wear. I remember getting really told off when one night I stuck a toe through a weak part of a sheet and tore it badly. My mother was terribly upset when she saw the tear.

CLOTHES, LINENS, AND LOOKING YOUR BEST

Clothing and all kinds of linens were rationed from the outbreak of the war to well after the war was over. Everything was marked with a little label to designate that it was indeed approved by whichever department was in charge of rationing. Perhaps the labels also served to prevent smuggling of some sort.

I still have a pair of towels that my Nan had managed to get during the war, white with two narrow red lines at top and bottom. They were of excellent quality and obviously were designed to last.

Clothing had a great impact on most people. When we visited the "Children of War" exhibition at the Imperial War Museum we saw, in a glass case, examples of clothing children wore. I immediately recognized a little boy's coat, the rough wool, the general appearance of the coat and the colour, a pale blue.

There used to be a clothing shop in Deptford High Street that sold ladies' clothes. It was where Mum bought her wedding dress, which she wore throughout the war and later. It was a double fronted shop and on one side the window display was of brightly coloured ladies' clothes but on the other side the clothes were all mourning clothes, mainly black but a few were dark purple. As the war went on and rationing grew ever more restrictive the mourning clothes side grew smaller. I suppose people were more willing to spend their clothing coupons on black clothing thinking they needed black coats and dresses more than brightly coloured clothes. Finally as the supply of clothing of all colours ran out one side of the shop was empty except for only a few items left being displayed in the window of that side of the shop.

At one time I had a pair of patent leather shoes, which must have been hand-me-downs as I can't imagine Mum wasting clothing coupons on something so fancy and impractical. These shoes had a strap that went across the top of the foot and fastened with a small button, which in turn was so small it had to be fastened with a button hook. This was a small hook with fancy handle I dreaded Mum or anyone else putting on my shoes because the button was so small that the button hook would pinch my feet, often quite painfully. I still have a problem with someone putting my shoes on for me, e.g. in a shoe shop. These button hooks were also used for fastening dresses or other garments; I can't imagine having someone else doing up a long line of buttons on the back of my dress. I still have the hated button hook, although I've never used it and hope I never will.

I used to have wavy blonde hair that people admired because it was almost white. Somehow my Mother got the idea that if she put ringlets in my hair I would look just like Shirley Temple. To achieve this she would put my hair up in curl papers or curl rags before I went to bed. These were terribly uncomfortable, digging into my head when I tried to sleep. They were supposed to curl my hair into lovely ringlets, when I complained Mum would tell me I had to suffer to be beautiful. Well I was sure I would never be beautiful and suffering like this simply wasn't worth it. Anyway the curls would drop out in a couple of hours so I never saw the point. I promised myself if I ever had a little girl I would never use the hated curl papers, and I never did.

THE STREET AND THE COALMAN

During the war our coal was rationed and my grandmother used to track the coal wagon when it came around to ask if they had any coal for us. This was not an easy task for although it seemed to me that there was some kind of list indicating when people were eligible for coal no-one followed it. One time we had a knock on the door and a coal man was standing on the step asking if we needed any coal. Of course we did, he went to great length to explain how he'd come across an extra ration of coal (one bag weighing a hundred weight of coal) and although it wasn't our turn to get a delivery, he didn't want to have to take it back to the yard. It was all very suspicious but we needed the coal so we took it.

The coal was then done up in smaller sacks and the coal men had to carry them through the house to get to the coal bin just outside the back door. The coal men were covered in coal dust and very dirty, so we were always asking them not to brush against the walls.

I was usually stationed in the front room to count the bags as they were carried in. Mum counted from the kitchen, and one day she said we'd been short changed. The men's response was "If you don't want it we'll take it back." Of course, we took it anyway.

It was always a gamble over the quality of the coal. Good coal burned neatly and well but quite often it was mixed with coke which burned but not nearly as well. Often a piece would explode in the fireplace with sometimes disastrous results. Sparks would fly out in many directions burning holes in the hearth rug that was kept in front of the fire. It was common to find holes or burn marks in every hearth rug around. For safety reasons we kept fire guards in front of every fire place, but despite this sparks would somehow explode over the top of the fire guard, thus burning yet more holes in the rug. At night time the fire would be tamped down with ashes to keep the fire burning very slowly so that it could be revived in the morning. If coal supplies were running low, as they too often were, the fires were simply put out at night.

There were other things that could be used on the fire. One was "Tarry Blocks," the wooden blocks that had been put in the streets to cover the cobblestones. They were covered in a thin layer of tarmac which wore down so it was decided to replace them and they were dug up and put on the side of the street. They had been soaked in tar and burned slowly but stunk to high heaven. Another job was to run out when a horse and cart went around the streets to follow these carts and to collect the (um, how should I put this?) whatever it was the horses left behind. This was burned too. I don't know how my grandmother knew all this, probably from her experiences in the First World War. But she did and it worked.

THE BUTCHER IN KEETONS ROAD

Meat was severely rationed, 4 oz. (1/4 pound) per person per week. I don't know if this influenced her decision, but one week Mum combined all our coupons and bought a roast of beef. Unfortunately, when it was cooked it shrank to the size of a small fist and was barely enough for four people to have a taste.

At any rate Mum decided to try a new butcher in Keetons Road, which was quite a long walk from the other butchers we normally went to.

It was a traditional butcher's shop, set on a corner with huge windows on either side of the door. These windows had no glass and were open to the elements, so the shop was always cold. Huge metal racks hung in the windows with hooks on which were displayed whatever meats the butcher had on hand. Usually the racks were empty, though I do remember a few pathetic rabbits with their feet tied together hanging there. At night wooden roller blinds would be pulled down and locked to protect the shop. Inside there were two marble-topped counters and a large wooden butcher's block for cutting up the meat. It had large hollows on the top from years of constant use. The floor was thickly covered in sawdust. Behind the counter was a large, heavy door, something like a bank vault door which led to the meat cooler.

There were two assistants and a butcher working in there. The butcher was a burly man, with large red, chapped hands and a 2 or 3 day growth of stubble on his face, he wore a large wrap around apron, which was always smeared with blood.

The first time we went he greeted Mum and showed her what meat was available, then he peered over the counter and said, "Oh there's my little girlfriend. I want a kiss." And before anyone could do or say anything he dashed around the counter, picked me up, hugged me and gave me a "kiss." It was not the kind of kiss I was used to from my family, though.

Instead he rubbed his unshaven cheek against mine. It scratched and hurt. It left my face chapped and sore. I hated it and I hated him.

On the way home I told Mum I didn't want to go back there but she just said he had told her he only shaved every other day because it was so cold and damp in the shop that shaving hurt his face. I couldn't argue with that even if I'd known how, but what about *my* face?

I was less than happy when we kept going back there. One day there was another mother with a little girl about my age going into the shop in front of us. When they reached the door the girl said she didn't want to go in and started to cry. Her mother tried to drag her in but finally told her to wait on the step. It was the first time I realized it wasn't just me he treated that way but probably every little girl who came to the shop got one of his "kisses."

Anyway, it didn't help; the butcher asked her mother where his little girlfriend was and came outside to pick her up and kissed her even though she was crying and screaming. Resistance, as they say, is futile.

One day I asked my grandmother why we went to that butchers when we had to pass other shops to get there. She replied That he was "the only butcher around who didn't weigh his thumb in with the meat." It was soon after that we stopped going to that particular shop, and nothing was ever said except for one time after the war when rationing restrictions were being lifted slightly. We were in my grandmother's kitchen and something was said about the butcher in Keetons Road. Suddenly my Aunt Olive burst out, "Oh, he is such a horrible little man," and looked at me.

Nothing more was said and I never brought it up, and now the opportunity has long passed for me to learn any more about it.

THE BRETON ONION SELLER

Contrast the Keetons Road experience with the day the Breton onion seller came to our door. He was a small, dark-haired man wearing a beret and holding a long string of onions with their tops plaited into a rope to hang them up with. We had seen the onion sellers going around the streets before so I knew who they were.

He handed Mum a card on which was written a few lines in English saying he was a onion seller from Brittany, and noting the price of the onion string. I couldn't read yet but Mum read it to me. I so wanted her to buy the onions, as they were so unlike the onions we got in the shops, but I knew they were too expensive and as Mum explained we couldn't use them all up before they went bad. She offered to buy just one but he couldn't or wouldn't pull one out of the string. I was so worried for him, wondering how he and his onions got from France to England and how he would get back to France. The coast was closed to civilians, the channel mined and blocked to all but military traffic, the beaches strewn with Dragon's Teeth (large concrete blocks in a triangular shape) to prevent tanks from landing and large middle sections cut out of every pier to prevent or at least delay the invasion. I imagined him rowing across the Channel at night to sell his onions.

All the time he had been talking to Mum he had been glancing at me and unable to reach a deal with Mum he turned to go. But before Mum could close the door he turned back and pulling out a battered wallet he opened it and showing a photo to Mum and using signs and considerably more English than he had first indicated he knew, asked if he could give me a hug. I pulled her arm down so I see the photo. It was of a little dark haired, dark eyed girl a little older than me.

Mum said gently, “This is his daughter, he misses her and he would like to give you a hug,” then perhaps mindful of my experience with the butcher, said, “Do you mind?” He picked me up and gave me a gentle hug but I was stiff and uncomfortable. Then he kissed me, to my surprise it was the merest brush of his lips, a light as the touch of a butterfly’s wing or the softest waft of a breeze. Then he put me down stroked my hair and walked away. As Mum closed the door I remarked what a funny man he was. Mum asked why I said that and I replied “When he h kissed me his face was all wet.”

THE TELEGRAM MESSENGER BOYS

The telegram messenger boys were a key part of the local communication system. They wore a snappy uniform and rode their single speed bikes with great proficiency. They usually whistled as they rode although many of the messages they delivered were undeserving of a happy tune. Through no fault of their own the messenger boys were seen as the carriers of bad news. The war office used the telegraph service to deliver messages to the kin of injured, missing or killed servicemen and women. It was not uncommon when a messenger boy entered a street for people to rush inside and lock their doors. The boy would come to the address and no one would answer the door. Often a neighbour would come to the boy's rescue, take the message and pay the fee. Probably the neighbour was relieved that the telegram wasn't for her.

The Wireless, the Programmes and the "Accumulators".

THE WIRELESS PROGRAMMES

The radio or wireless was of vital importance during the war years. For most people it was the only reliable source available for information about the war.

Newspapers were often unreliable, sometimes being late or not appearing at all depending on the availability or delivery of newsprint. But the radio was always there, with the news of the happenings of the day.

The newscasts always started with the announcer giving his or her full name and the name of the service, the British Broadcasting Commission. One day I asked my Dad why they did that and he told me it was in case of an invasion, so everyone would know there was a problem if the routine varied. The newscasts were always sombre with news of air raids around the country. It would end with news of retaliatory raids against Germany giving the number of planes involved in the raids and ending with the line, "Two, *or another number*, of our aircraft are missing." One night the grim announcement was that fourteen of our aircraft are missing. My grandmother said softly "There'll be tears tonight." I didn't understand what she meant 'til many years later.

I enjoyed most of the programmes, especially "Children's Hour" which ran daily from 5 to 6 PM and was hosted by Uncle Mac, who had a wonderful speaking voice and a warm personality that came across the airwaves. Lots of other children thought so too and wrote to ask for a photo of him; he always replied with a charming letter and an excuse, he was waiting for more photos to come in or something similar. It wasn't until much later that word got out that there were no photos of him and never would be. Uncle Mac had been an air force pilot who was shot down early in the war and terribly burned. He had refused to have to have his photo taken fearing it would scare the smaller children. But I had a picture in my mind of him — tall, slim and very handsome, all based on the sound of his voice — I didn't need a photo.

The radio was on all day, providing a backdrop to our lives. There were music programmes in the mornings and early afternoon — *Workers Playtime* for example — which played the popular pop tunes of the day. Then came *Children's Hour*, then a lengthy newscast at 6 PM and then the evening shows.

Much Binding in the Marsh was set in an isolated air base deep in the country and, as were all the programmes of the day, filled with catch phrases. The lead characters would turn on the radio for the news at the beginning of the show and then say "It takes a long while to warm up." It would take to the end of the show before they would get any information on "their fictional wireless."

Probably the most popular show was *It's That Man Again*, starring Tommy Handley and featuring a cast of unlikely characters, the most famous being Mrs. Mopp, the cleaner, who spent most of the programme moaning about everything and closing with her famous line, "Its being so cheerful wot keeps me going."

Tommy Handley died shortly after the war ended; his death was put down to stress. He had poked fun mercilessly at Hitler and his generals and it became known that Hitler had given an order that following the invasion of the UK, Handley was to be taken alive. One can only imagine the fate Hitler had in mind for him. Tommy Handley was given a state funeral, something unheard of for an ordinary civilian. It was granted in recognition of his work during the war in maintaining the morale of the British citizenry.

Another favourite saying was Arthur Askey's "Is your journey really necessary?"

Askey hosted a series of radio shows during the war. Mum and I actually met him once. One day in Great Milton we were walking to the railway station, quite a distance from the cottage or so it seemed for my little legs, when a large black car drew up beside us a window rolled down and Mr. Askey asked if we needed a lift. Naturally we said "Yes!" and scrambled into the car. It was very large with two jump seats on one side where Mr. Askey and his daughter Anthea were sitting. His daughter was in a very bad mood and sat staring out of the window, ignoring us completely. Mr. Askey was very charming and went to great lengths to explain to us that he got extra petrol coupons so he could drive up to London for his shows. I think he meant to drive us all the way to London but maybe because of his daughter's attitude he dropped us at the station and drove away. Whatever the reason, we were very grateful for the lift.

OUR WIRELESS AND ITS ACCUMULATORS

Our wireless was formidable object in itself, a large wooden cabinet which sat on a table against one of the walls. By today's standards it took up a great amount of space in our back room. But the most remarkable thing about it was that it was battery driven, oh no, not the small double or triple As so familiar today but rechargeable batteries called accumulators. These were large glass containers filled with acid and lead plates which had to be removed from the back of the wireless and taken to a radio shop to be recharged. They were heavy normally but ours were even heavier because the two cells were physically combined. They had to be carried all the way by foot since most of the bus drivers wouldn't allow us to take them on their buses in case the acid was spilled. It took at least 24 hours to recharge them and then we had to go back and carry them home again. Oh they were so heavy! All the while, Mum would be cautioning me not to spill any acid on myself, on my clothes or anything else.

A table top wireless

Courtesy: The Museum of Technology

A double wet-celled. wireless accumulator

Courtesy: The Museum of Technology

More Wartime Memories

SIGNS AND SLOGANS

There were many signs around the streets, posted on buses, trains and lamp standards. They were generally on the lines of "Loose lips sink ships" or "Turn off your lights." The latter was a sticky label which could be placed by a light switch.

Mostly I didn't pay too much notice of them as they were just background to my life. They applied to something adults were supposed to take care of.

But the one I really remember is one that annoyed me very much. It read "Is your journey really necessary?" Mostly it was used on trains. I used to think if it wasn't necessary, would we be going anywhere? I suppose it was meant to help conserve fuel.

Though I had completely forgotten about it until recently, there was one poster which made a great impact on me. I'm sure everyone has seen it in one form or another and has maybe even made fun of it. This poster now reads "Keep calm and carry on." The first time I saw it recently I instantly remembered the complete version and the whole emotional impact came rushing back. The original was in white print on a red ground and it read,

"In case of INVASION, keep calm and carry on."

The complete version makes a great deal more sense, for at the time an invasion was a very real threat. The Axis were massed on the French coast, only 22 miles away from England's shore. I believe it is difficult for people in North America to appreciate the daily stress that the citizens of Great Britain experienced. We were, in a sense, living literally within shooting distance of the enemy.

THE BIRDS THAT SANG

During the war my Grandmother had a beautiful canary called Billy. He had a lovely song with which he would entertain us frequently.

At night his cage would be covered with a cloth so he could sleep. Unfortunately no one bothered to tell Billy this and during air raids he would sing at the top of his voice until the raid stopped. My Nan always said she thought he was sending coded messages to Hitler.

But he wasn't the only bird who sang during air raids. There is a famous recording made by a reporter who went into the country somewhere close to London to try to get a recording of a skylark singing. He found such a skylark but during the recording an air raid started, in lulls between the sirens, the bombs exploding and the guns firing can be heard the beautiful song of the skylark. The recording became famous as a symbol of defiance during the war.

Kind People and A Memorable Celebration

GOLDEN GROVE

Sometime during the latter third of the war, Mum got letter saying the Dad was posted to a place in Wales called Golden Grove for training prior to being posted overseas. This was followed by a notice saying we could travel to Golden Grove to visit Dad before he left. We could only stay one day and because of the difficulties of travel it would have been impossible for us to get to this place and get home again in one day. Then a few days later we got another letter saying the lady who owned the house which had been taken over by the RAF had retained one wing of it for her family to live in and insisted that anyone with small children be allowed to stay for two or three days. All I can think is that she must have been an extremely forceful character. Mum jumped at the chance and we travelled to Wales, a long and difficult journey. The owner showed herself to be a very kind and caring person. She met with all of us asking if there was anything we needed and on Sunday there was a church service and she asked all the small children for their favourite hymns to play at the service. I was very shy but managed to tell her *All Things Bright and Beautiful* was my favourite and it was played, to my delight.

In the afternoon we went for a walk — Mum, Dad, and me — through the woods surrounding the house. I was walking ahead and suddenly stopped because a large fox with a most impressive brush had started across the path and stopped to look at me. Even today in my mind's eye I can still see that magnificent fox.

REMEMBRANCE DAY

On this Remembrance Day, as I have for years I will be thinking of one particular man. I do not know his name, in fact I do not remember meeting him but every year I think of a small gesture that became a family legend.

I know the story because it was the only war experience my mother ever talked about. It happened at London Bridge railway station early in the war when I was very tiny. I don't know where we coming from or where we were going but half way up the dank, damp stone staircase leading from Duke St. Hill to the station forecourt the air raid sirens sounded and almost immediately came the sounds of planes overhead and the thud of bombs exploding. My mother picked me up and ran up the stairs to the station forecourt which was a terminus for the double- decker buses as well as trains. The semi-circular forecourt was lined with shops with double fronted windows, deep doorways and overhung with a wide span of tempered glass. The noise and smells were terrible: Ack-Ack guns were firing, the dreadful roar of the bombers flying over head, the thunder of the explosions. Plus the air was filled with dust and the smells of cordite.

Mum ducked into one of these doorways with me, terrified and screaming in her arms. There was one other person in the doorway, a policeman who had also taken shelter there. There was probably an air raid shelter in the station but it would have been madness to try to reach it. Mum tried to soothe me but I was nearly hysterical with fright and beyond soothing.

In those days people in essential jobs — firemen, air raid wardens and policemen — were issued an extra ration of chocolate bars to keep up their energy. They were not the sort of chocolate bars so familiar today. These bars were thin — mere slivers really — with six little squares of fairly unpalatable chocolate. But with all sweets being strictly rationed they were something civilians rarely, if ever, saw.

According to my mother as I cried on inconsolably the policeman reached into a pocket, pulled out one of these chocolate bars and handed it to Mum saying "Here, missus, give this to her, she needs it more than I do," and then he walked out of the doorway in search of other shelter or to carry on his duties.

Although I don't remember this, but since we lived in the area and I became so familiar with the station I can visualize the whole incident. I have but a fleeting impression of my mother trying to quiet me by putting something unfamiliar in my mouth. It was the taste of chocolate mixed with the saltiness of tears.

We did not know the policeman, his name or anything about him but every Remembrance Day I think of him and his generosity, and I say a silent "thank you."

VE DAY, MAY 15, 1945

I was three months short from being seven and the excitement that swept over the country when the news came that the war was over was palpable.

We heard on the wireless that the church of St. Martin-in-the-Fields was holding continuous services of thanksgiving that day. While we had all been caught in countless air raids no one in the family had been injured or killed and while my father and other members of the family were still serving overseas they too had survived.

So we, Nan, Mum, and I, went up to St Martin to give thanks. We had to get off the bus on Waterloo Bridge — there were so many people on the streets that the bus drivers were abandoning their buses in the middle of the streets and joining the crowds. Everyone was hugging everyone else.

Somehow we got to the church but it was so packed we couldn't get in. People were spilling out and others crowding close to the doors trying to hear the service. We turned around and looked out over Trafalgar Square, down the Mall to Buckingham Palace and down Whitehall towards the river. Nowhere could we see a square inch of pavement — everywhere was a packed mass of people hugging, laughing, crying, singing & dancing. We tried to get down the Mall to the Palace but it was impossible so we turned around, walked through the happy crowds who only wanted to gather and share their joy at the marvellous news. We finally crossed Waterloo Bridge, caught a bus and made our way home.

An abandoned bus and a massive crowd in the Strand

I don't think I've experienced the like since. It was the most massive display of ***Collective Joy*** one could ever imagine.

The pubs in England always had rigid opening and closing rules but on VE Day there were no rules. The pubs were open all up and down the Strand and I am sure elsewhere as well.

EPILOGUE

The writing of ***Teddy and Me, The Blitz and other Childhood War Memories***, was an exciting and incredibly revealing process. It was exciting because I was greatly surprised by the number of childhood memories that came forth. But it was also self revealing.

It was then that I started to piece together these childhood memories, some of my life experiences, my history of health issues, and some of the brain research my husband studied. I began to realize that my current health problems, might very well stem from the stresses, fears, and uncertainties that I encountered as a wartime child.

After years of experiencing, and being treated for, a variety of ailments it was finally thought that I might have Lupus. After undergoing some extensive laboratory work my Rheumatologist, put to rest any uncertainty by saying "Your condition was analyzed on four separate tests, a positive result on any one would suggest you might have Lupus, you scored positive on all four of them."

Lupus is an autoimmune disease which attacks the connective tissues within the body and each individual is affected wholly or slightly differently. Lupus like most other human conditions is the result of the interaction of one's genetics and environment. The old question used to be is it nature or nurture? The new answer is that it is nature ***and*** nurture.

The emotional energy expenditure of writing *Teddy 'N' Me* and the subsequent surfacing of the seven decades old memories may have been the cause of the one of the most severe Lupus flare-ups I have ever experienced.

Wars may have start and stop dates but they don't have on and off switches for the brains and bodies of those who have suffered either as armed services personnel or civilians. For example almost daily we hear of service personnel and ex-service personnel who suffer from Post Traumatic Stress Disorder (PTSD). Brain scans of people experiencing PTSD show inner brain regions being unexpectedly over active even though the person is in a safe, restful environment.

Research is clearly showing the adverse relationships between trauma and a variety of health issues.

People who have not fought in a war, who have not been in areas targeted for bombing or strafing, or who have not endured hunger or other forms of deprivation caused by war are seldom able to know the full impact of war. On Remembrance Days we pay homage to the thousands upon thousands of men and women who died in combat and so we should, but we haven't and still don't pay as much attention to the men and women who came home but never left the military hospitals or who lived the remainder of their lives physically limited and/or mentally tormented by the images of war which they couldn't shake. This also applies to the civilians, young and old, who experienced the noise, the smells, the fires, and the host of other human stresses and tensions of war.

Although it has been suspected for some time, it is only now been understood, to some reasonable level, that many memories of war or other trauma are not language-based but rather are buried deep within our emotional memory system and these memories may be triggered at unexpected times and in confusing ways.

In my case incidents which triggered these memories include:

- **The Children of War Exhibit** evoked several "long forgotten" reactions to bombing raids and times spent in air raid shelters.

- **Rene's Christmas Parcels** allows me to think about the love, generosity and self-sacrifice that were embodied in each of those treasured gifts.

- **Collective Joy.** Mary Hynes in her CBC "Tapestry" programme gave me this two-word phrase to capture the massive euphoria of victory, feeling of unity, and release of stress as thousands upon thousands of people came together that afternoon and evening in the heart of London on VE Day. Collective Joy **is** the perfect phrase.

- **Barrage Balloons**. It still amazes me that the sight of a single, relatively small barrage balloon flying high over a flat prairie landscape could evoke such a strong reactive response.

- **Crossing the Iron Grating on a Winnipeg Bridge** and my reaction. This highlights how a hidden childhood memory can cause much anxiety and discomfort well into adulthood.

- **Evacuations, while necessary, were emotionally unsettling events.** People had to leave their homes in the city and move out into the country to live with strangers in very unfamiliar environments. I thought the quiet of the country was a godsend but I am sure my mother had more trouble adapting and worried daily about her mother and their home in London.

THE AUTHOR

Peggy Halstead was born Peggy Grace Collins in London, England on a mid August Thursday in 1938 less than 13 months before Britain declared war against Germany. She was a child of the war. Air raid sirens, Ack-Ack guns being fired, barrage balloons flying overhead, search lights probing the night sky, bombs being dropped nearby, twice being evacuated and her father being in service and away from home. These were her childhood realities. She spent countless hours, in the air raid shelter in her Nan Collins's garden or having her afternoon naps in an indoor one.

In **"TEDDY 'N' ME, The Blitz and other Childhood War Memories"** she shares her childhood memories. After the war, she, like thousands of other children of the war tried to get on with life as best as they could. She completed secondary school, worked for the Bank of England and then British Overseas Airways Corporation known, in jest, amongst the staff as (Better On A Camel). In 1963 she immigrated to Canada for a one year work term and 51 years later she is still there, married to David, mother of Neal and Sara, Nana to Nathaniel, Melissa, Anja, Isaac and Eden. She has 16 years experience as an elected public school trustee in two cities.

Her writings have included material for: Regional and National CBC Radio, Regina Leader Post, RCMP Quarterly, Peter Gzowski's "About This Country in the Morning", a number of other Canadian and United States publications and, most recently, Stuart McLean's book "Time Now For The Vinyl Cafe Story Exchange". In addition she has three film scripts to her credit.

Her travels have taken her to four of the five continents and she has lived in England, Canada and Ghana, West Africa.

It was during the past decade as she worked alongside David, as he probed the research on brain development including the role emotions play in childhood development, that she realized she had valuable stories to tell. Central to her stories are the war emotions of: terror, near constant fear, anger and uncertainty. She now understands the impact these emotions had on her very early childhood and how they still affect her even today.

CRITICAL HISTORIC DATES

- 1939 — September 3, 1939. Great Britain, Australia, New Zealand and France declare war on Germany.
- 1939 — September 10, 1939 Canada declares war on Germany.
- 1940 — July to October 1940, the aerial Battle of Britain, a decisive win for RAF.
- 1940 — September 7, 1940 to May 16, 1941 "The Blitz", London was bombed 71 days and nights with one stretch of 57 consecutive nights.
- 1940 — Evacuation of Dunkirk May 27 - June 4, 1940
- 1941 — December 11, 1941 The United States declares war on Germany.
- 1944 — June 6, 1944, D-Day, Allied invasion of France
- 1944 — June 13, 1944 to October 1944 London besieged by V-1 rockets, the Buzz Bombs
- 1944-45 — September 8, 1944 to March 27, 1945, London attacked by the V-2 Rockets
- **1945 — May 15 — VE Day**

Printed in Canada